About Mastering Basic Skills—Listening Skills:

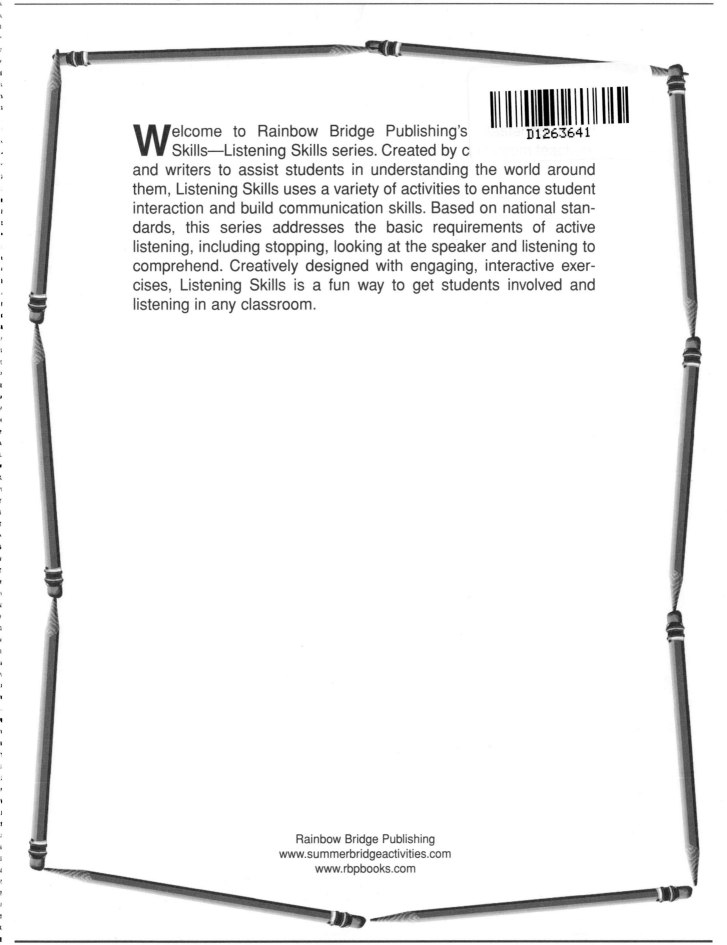

Welcome to Rainbow Bridge Publishing's Skills—Listening Skills series. Created by c and writers to assist students in understanding the world around them, Listening Skills uses a variety of activities to enhance student interaction and build communication skills. Based on national standards, this series addresses the basic requirements of active listening, including stopping, looking at the speaker and listening to comprehend. Creatively designed with engaging, interactive exercises, Listening Skills is a fun way to get students involved and listening in any classroom.

Rainbow Bridge Publishing
www.summerbridgeactivities.com
www.rbpbooks.com

Listening Skills • Table of Contents

◇ Start Here!

Teacher: Read the story and the instructions aloud to the students.

The hot August sun blazed in the sky as Denise lay beneath the old oak tree in her backyard. Spread around her were several journals. She wrote in them every day. Today she was rereading passages from the past three years. She was surprised how much she had changed since her first days in kindergarten. In three short years she had learned to write in complete sentences and was getting pretty good at cursive. She knew most of her multiplication tables and loved to read aloud to her younger brother.

Denise's favorite subject in school was science. Last year she had had some problems with a few experiments that she and her classmates had done at school. Her teacher told Denise to practice her listening skills over the summer. "I might as well review them now," thought Denise. "It's really too hot to do anything else."

Here is what Denise thought about:

S: I know I am to <u>stop</u> doing whatever I might be doing when a teacher starts explaining science experiments.

E: Next, I should <u>empty</u> my hands of anything I am holding, because I might fiddle around and not pay attention.

L: I should <u>look</u> at my teacher because it helps me stay focused.

L: I need to <u>listen</u> carefully to any lesson or instructions and ask questions if I am unsure of what I am supposed to do.

"Now I just need to be sure to practice those steps in third grade so I don't foul up any more experiments," said Denise to herself.

1 **Group Activity:** Write directions for a three-step activity (i.e., clap your hands twice, draw a circle, then stand on your right foot). Read all three directions to a classmate, and see if he or she can follow them exactly. Read the directions only once. Then switch and follow your classmate's directions.

◇Start Here!

Teacher: Copy the accompanying picture. Then read the story and the instructions to the students.

Before school started in September, Denise and her family were going on a trip to Canada. Since June, Denise and her father had been studying maps to figure out the most scenic way to drive to Montreal and Quebec City. Also, her mother and older brother had sent for information about different historical sites to visit and good places to eat. Denise had learned so much about Canada over the summer, she could hardly wait to visit!

1 The Canadian province (or state) of Quebec is located north of the United States. Circle the maple leaf that reads NORTH.

2 Quebec is twice the size of Texas. Color the sign that reads Texas GREEN.

3 Quebec City and Montreal are Quebec's two largest cities. Write a word that rhymes with TWO on the blank menu.

4 Canada was claimed by France in 1534. The land was called New France. Find the crown in the tree and color it PURPLE.

5 Later, France and Britain fought a war to decide which country would own Canada. France lost. Put a frowny face on the table.

6 However, even today, Quebec keeps its French ways. Ninety-eight out of one hundred people speak French. In fact, Montreal is the second largest French-speaking city in the world. The first is Paris. Color the sign that reads "Only French Spoken Here" LIGHT PINK.

7 The Canadian flag has two red outer stripes with a white middle section. The maple leaf in the center of the flag is red. Color Canada's Flag.

8 Maple trees can be found almost everywhere in the province of Quebec. Color the maple tree using RED, ORANGE and BROWN.

9 In March, workers put a tap, similar to a kitchen faucet, into the maple trees and collect the tree's sap. This sap is used to make maple syrup for your pancakes and many other tasty food items. Find the faucet and color it BLACK.

Name _____   Date_____

ONLY
FRENCH
SPOKEN
HERE.

MENU

TEXAS
STREET

NORTH

France
Loses War

◇ **Start Here!**

Teacher: Copy the accompanying picture. Then read the story and the instructions to the students.

"Denise," Mom said. "You received a postcard from Florida today. I think it is from Sarah."

"Yea!" said Denise. "She promised to tell me all about her trip." Denise sat down to read the card. "She says that she had fun at Walt Disney World and at the beach. She has seen lots of palm trees and orange trees, and she even saw an alligator!"

"Sounds exciting," Mom said. "Let's see what else we can learn about Florida, and then you can ask Sarah some questions when she comes home."

---

1 Florida's nickname is "the Sunshine State" because its climate is so warm. Many people go to Florida to play on the beautiful beaches and enjoy the famous sunshine. Color the sun YELLOW.

2 Florida's state tree is the sabal palm tree. Parts of the tree are used for food and medicine. Also, Seminole Indians used to use the palm leaves to make roofs for their houses. Color the palm leaves GREEN and the trunk BROWN.

3 Florida produces more oranges than any other country besides Brazil. Over 90 percent of all the oranges grown in Florida are squeezed to make orange juice. Color the orange ORANGE. An orange is a type of citrus fruit. Florida also produces other citrus fruits, such as grapefruits. Grapefruits do not taste like grapes at all. Grapefruits get their funny name because they grow on trees in clusters, like a bunch of grapes. Draw a grapefruit next to the orange and color it YELLOW.

4 When Spanish explorers settled here, they called the area Florida because of all the flowers. Florida is a Spanish word for flowers. Draw a FLOWER next to the orange.

5 Florida is famous for having lots of alligators. The alligators often hide in swamps. Adult alligators can be up to 12 feet long! Alligators can move surprisingly fast, and their powerful jaws make them dangerous creatures. Mother alligators are especially dangerous when they are protecting their nests. Draw THREE eggs next to the alligator.

6 Many dolphins live off the coasts of Florida. There are places in Florida where you can pay to swim with the dolphins. Sailors used to believe that if dolphins swam by their boat, it was a sign of good luck. Draw a BOAT next to the dolphin.

7 Florida is also home to many amusement parks. Many of the parks are in the cities of Orlando or Kissimmee. Draw a LINE from Orlando to Kissimmee and color the Ferris wheel BLUE.

Name _____ Date _____

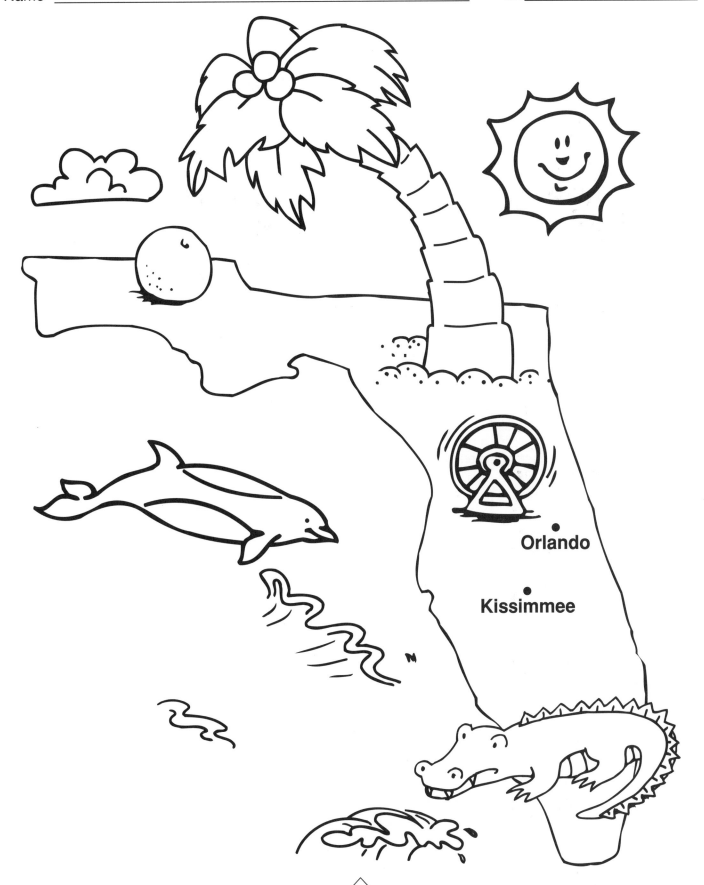

Orlando

Kissimmee

www.rbpbooks.com   reproducible   **MBS—Listening Skills Grade 3**

⬦ **Start Here!**

Teacher: Read the instructions and the story aloud to the students.

I'm going to hand you a piece of paper. When you get it, write your first and last name on the top line. Next, write the numbers 1–7 down the left-hand side of the paper. Then, put your pencil down and get ready to listen to a story.

Alexander Graham Bell was born in Edinburgh, Scotland, in 1847. He is best known for inventing the telephone with help from his assistant, Thomas Watson.

When Alexander was 23, he moved to Canada with his family. One year later he moved to the United States, where he taught deaf students at a school in Boston. Later, he married a deaf woman named Mabel Hubbard.

In 1875 Alexander began experimenting with thin, steel tubes. He wanted to find out if his assistant Watson could hear his voice from far away. It took the two of them less than one year to figure out how to vibrate steel rods along an electrical wire with their voices. By 1876 Bell and Watson were speaking clearly to each other with one in the attic and the other in the basement. Alexander Bell's first words to Watson were "Mr. Watson. Come here. I want you."

Alexander Graham Bell died at age 75 after a lifetime of developing wonderful inventions. In honor of Bell, all phones in the United States were turned off for one minute on the day he was buried.

Listen closely as I read each question, then write the letter that gives the best answer.

1 What was Alexander Bell most famous for?
    A. inventing the hydrofoil   B. teaching the deaf   C. inventing the telephone

2 Bell was born in
    A. Scotland   B. United States   C. Canada

3 Who was Bell's assistant?
    A. Mabel   B. Watson   C. Helen Keller

4 What did Bell use to help create the telephone?
    A. steel rods and electrical wire   B. rope and a tin can   C. steel tubes and rope

5 Mabel, Bell's wife, was
    A. blind   B. deaf   C. deaf and blind

6 How old was Alexander when he died?
    A. 50 years old   B. 75 years old   C. 85 years old

7 Write a title for the story. _____

This origami is easier than it looks. After only a few tries your students will be making cups from every scrap of paper they can find. Ordinary copy paper will actually hold water, and a supervised trip to the drinking fountain provides a nice break at the end of this lesson.

 1 Fold a square sheet of paper (8" x 8") in half.

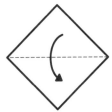

 2 Fold down one side. Then unfold.

 3 Fold left corner to fold line on opposite side.

 4 Fold right corner to corner on opposite side.

 5 Fold one layer of top corner down. Turn over and repeat.

 6 Wiggle fingers on the inside to open up the cup. Enjoy!

◇ **Start Here!**

Teacher: See page 32 for directions.

 Why do I sneeze?

Your body has many different ways of protecting itself from germs, poisons and chemicals. When you sneeze, your body is getting rid of dust, plant pollens and scents such as pepper or perfumes. Your brain sends a signal to your lungs to shoot out a large amount of air through your nose. Hurry and get a tissue, because the air is moving out your nose at about one hundred miles per hour!

 What is a germ?

A germ is a virus or bacteria. These little creatures are so small you need a microscope to see them. They live everywhere on earth and on you! Some of the billions of germs that you come in contact with each day could cause you to feel ill. Germs can get inside your body through a cut in your skin, eating food that is not clean or by breathing air when someone has coughed or sneezed nearby. The most common virus that makes you sick is the cold virus. Covering your mouth and nose when you sneeze or cough and washing your hands before you eat will help prevent illness and keep your own germs from spreading.

 Why do I have a bellybutton?

Before you were born, a small tube containing blood vessels joined you to your mother. This special tube brought oxygen and other nutrients to you to help you grow into a strong baby. After you were born, you didn't need the tube anymore, so the doctor who delivered you cut it off. Don't worry! The tube, or umbilical cord, doesn't have any nerves, so you didn't feel a thing. Your bellybutton is where the tube was attached to you.

 Why do I have skin?

Skin is like a big, huge bag that covers your entire body. It holds your insides in and keeps the outside out. It is a little thicker than a computer disc. Skin has blood vessels and nerve endings in it. When you get cut, the nerves in your skin send a message to your brain that says, "Ouch! Something bad is happening." Hair and sweat come from the skin. When you get too hot, holes, or pores, in your skin release salty water to help your body temperature go back down.

⬧ **Start Here!**

Teacher: Read the instructions and the story aloud to the students.

I'm going to hand you a piece of paper. When you get it, write your first and last name on the top line. Next, write the numbers 1–7 down the left-hand side of the paper. Then, put your pencil down and get ready to listen to a story.

In 1770 a little boy named Ludwig van Beethoven was born in Germany. His father, a grumpy man, would return home late at night and drag little Ludwig out of bed, forcing him to practice the piano until the early hours of the morning. You see, Ludwig's father wanted him to be a famous pianist and play for the royal family.

At age 17, Ludwig moved away from his family to Vienna, a gorgeous city in Austria where many great music teachers and composers lived. Friends of the talented Mozart asked him to instruct Beethoven on the piano. At first Mozart refused. Mozart, who was always neat and well dressed, thought Ludwig was a sloppy man with his uncombed black hair and messy clothes. However, after hearing Beethoven play, Mozart exclaimed, "Watch this young man. Someday he will force the world to talk about him."

And indeed he did! By age 25, Ludwig was composing for kings and queens. Even though he wrote music for royalty, he enjoyed himself most when playing for the common people (people who were not rich or royal). Everyone loved to hear Beethoven's music, and his concerts were always "sold out."

Unfortunately, by age 30, Ludwig began to lose his hearing. He continued writing and playing beautiful music. His friends learned to talk to Ludwig by writing in notebooks, which Ludwig then read.

When Ludwig van Beethoven died at age 57, about 30,000 people lined the streets of Vienna to watch as his coffin was carried to the cemetery.

Listen closely as I read each question; then write the letter that gives the best answer.

1 What word best describes Ludwig's father?
    A. happy   B. sad   C. grumpy

2 Who was asked to teach Beethoven?
    A. Bach   B. Mozart   C. Copeland

3 Which best describes Beethoven?
    A. sloppy, messy, talented   B. neat, well dressed, talented   C. grumpy, rich, talented

4 About how many people lined the streets when Beethoven died?
    A. 300   B. 3,000   C. 30,000

5 How did his friends "talk" to Beethoven after he lost his hearing?
    A. by talking louder   B. by writing in a notebook   C. Beethoven read their lips.

6 In what city did Beethoven die?
    A. Vienna   B. England   C. Germany

7 Write a title for this story. _____

◇ **Start Here!**

Teacher: Copy the accompanying picture. Then read the story and the instructions to the students.

(Note: Write "Orville and Wilbur Wright" on the chalkboard before the lesson.)

"Can you help me find some books about people who invented the airplane?" Denise asked the librarian. "I want to fly to Washington, D.C., with my dad to see the National Air and Space Museum, but I've never flown on a plane. I'm a little nervous."
"I have just the book you need," said Mr. Johns, the librarian.

---

 1 About 130 years ago, two brothers named Wilbur and Orville Wright were growing up in the United States. Write WILBUR on the sweatshirt of one boy and ORVILLE on the other.

 2 They enjoyed building kites after school and flying them high above the corn and wheat fields on the outskirts of their hometown, Dayton, Ohio. Write a word that rhymes with KITE on the kite.

 3 After receiving a toy helicopter from their father at Christmas, the two boys played with it constantly. It was an unusual toy back then, because working helicopters hadn't yet been made. By studying the propeller on the toy helicopter, Wilbur and Orville were able to build similar toys. After measuring how long the toys were able to stay in the air, the boys began to improve on the propeller design. Color the propellers on the plane BLACK. Then count how many blades are on both propellers and write that number on the SUN.

 4 When the Wright brothers were in their early twenties, they opened a shop where they built and sold bicycles. This became important because the brothers used bikes when they began experimenting with gliders. What SHAPE is a bicycle tire? Draw that shape below the sun.

 5 A glider is a light plane without an engine. It uses wind power to fly. In 1900, Wilbur and Orville flew their first glider at Kitty Hawk, North Carolina. Write NC on the SAND DUNE.

 6 By watching how birds flew over the beach and ocean, Wilbur and Orville were able to improve the wing design. By the time their lives were over, they had plans for over 200 types of wings. Write 200 on the sea gull.

 7 Adding a gasoline engine that powered two propellers to a glider allowed the two brothers to finally soar in the air. In 1903, using a plane called <u>Flyer</u>, Orville flew 40 yards, or the length of half a football field. Soon after, Wilbur flew <u>Flyer</u> 284 yards, or the length of three football fields. Write the name of the Wright brothers' first plane above the plane.

Name _____ Date _____

Teacher: Read the instructions; then read the directions aloud to the students.

Making these origami houses will not only help with looking and listening skills, but they can be used to make fascinating neighborhood habitats. Have the students decorate them to resemble fire stations, homes, bakeries, libraries and so on. Team up and be creative.

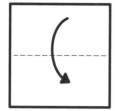 **1** Fold a square (8" x 8") in half. Then fold it in half again.

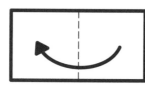

 4 A 3-d house can be made by folding peaked sections out to the sides.

Have fun making an entire village.

 2 Unfold the second fold; then fold outer edges to the center.

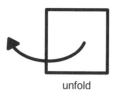

unfold

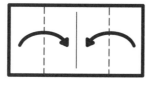

 3 Unfold the fold made in step 2. Pull B and C apart while squashing A flat. Repeat on other end.

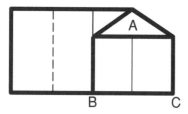

◇ Start Here!

Teacher: Read the instructions and the story aloud to the students.

I'm going to hand you a piece of paper. When you get it, write your first and last name on the top line. Next, write the numbers 1–7 down the left-hand side of the paper. Then, put your pencil down and get ready to listen to a story.

Once upon a time, there was a king named Midas, who loved gold more than anything else in the world. Sometimes he thought a glistening coin was more lovely than his wife, Marigold, or his sweet, young daughter, Hollyhock.

One day, a stranger dressed in rich robes came to visit King Midas at his castle. "Midas, you are indeed a wealthy man," said the stranger as he sipped tea from a golden teacup while sitting on a golden chair in a golden room.

"Alas, it seems I am," answered Midas. "But I would need to live another hundred years to collect enough gold to be truly happy. I only wish that everything I touched turned to gold."

A sad look danced across the stranger's face as he rose to leave. "Are you sure that this is what you wish for?" When Midas nodded, the stranger said, "So be it. Tomorrow you will awake with the Golden Touch." Almost as quickly as he had come, the stranger disappeared through the castle gates.

The king slept badly that evening. He tossed and turned as he dreamt of golden rings and coins, dishes and pots, vases and mirrors, thrones and crowns. The poor man woke in the morning with quite a headache. Princess Hollyhock raced into her parents' bedroom, as was her way each day. "Good morning, Father," she said, throwing her arms around his neck. Before the words were out of her mouth, Hollyhock transformed into a solid, gold statue.

"What have you done?" cried Queen Marigold. In a moment, she too was turned to gold.

In horror, Midas fled from his castle in search of the stranger who had given him such a terrible curse. As you might guess, peasants and princes alike would run from Midas rather than risk his deadly touch.

It is said that Midas died soon after. You see, even apples off a tree became golden when he tried to eat them.

Listen closely as I read each question; then write the letter that gives the best answer.

1. What killed Midas?   A. a disease   B. hunger   C. his wife

2. What was Midas's daughter's name?   A. Marigold   B. Goldy   C. Hollyhock

3. Why did Midas have a headache?   A. because he dreamt all night
   B. because his golden crown was too heavy   C. because his wife yelled at him

4. What danced across the stranger's face?   A. a ballerina   B. a golden light   C. a sad look

5. When Midas fled the castle, what was he looking for?   A. a prince   B. a stranger   C. a peasant

6. What would happen to everyone King Midas touched?   A. They turned to gold.   B. They became ill.
   C. They became King.

7. Write a title for "The Deadly Touch." _____

◇ **Start Here!**

Teacher: Copy the accompanying picture. Then read the story and the instructions to the students.

"Mom, why are there dots beneath the floor numbers on the elevator?" asked Denise.

"Good question," said Mom. "They're a form of writing called Braille. People who are blind read the floor numbers by running their fingers over the dots."

"Tell me more," said Denise.

Note: Before reading the questions below, introduce your students to the Braille alphabet on the next page. Explain that placing dots in a certain order, in a space of three places down and two spaces across, creates each letter of the alphabet.

---

1. Two hundred years ago, in a small village in France, a young boy named Louis Braille had a terrible accident while playing in his father's workshop. On line #1 write THREE in Braille.

2. Louis was playing with sharp tools, tools he had been told never to touch. He slipped and a tool injured his left eye so badly, he lost his sight. An infection spread from his left eye and caused him to go blind in his right eye also. On line #2 write EYE in Braille.

3. In the time Louis lived, most blind people led very difficult lives. Many begged for food on street corners or lived in poorhouses because they couldn't see to work. Write MONEY in Braille on line #3.

4. Louis's parents loved him very much and wanted as normal a life as possible for him. His sister, Catherine, taught him his ABCs by forming the alphabet out of sticks and straw. This way Louis could feel the raised letters, but it was impossible for whole books to be made out of straw letters. On line #4 write STRAW in Braille.

5. From age six to ten Louis went to the village school and was tutored by the local priest. He was an excellent student, who remembered each daily lesson almost perfectly. Louis was extremely bright at math and solved problems quickly in his head. However, he was always frustrated that he couldn't read. On line #5 write the words READ in Braille.

6. When Louis was ten his parents made the hard choice to send him to Paris to attend the National Institute for the Young Blind. On line #6 write SCHOOL in Braille.

7. Two years later, when Louis was 12, he began to create the method of punching holes in leather to make a series of raised dots that represented each letter of the alphabet. By the time he was 15 he was copying whole books for his fellow students (a sighted person read the books aloud to Louis). Louis spent the rest of his life at the Institute teaching other blind students how to read using Braille. On line #7 write TWELVE in Braille.

Name _____   Date_____

| a | b | c | d | e | f | g | h | i | j | k | l | m |

| n | o | p | q | r | s | t | u | v | w | x | y | z |

1. _____

2. _____

3. _____

4. _____

5. _____

6. _____

7. _____

 Start Here!

Teacher: Read the instructions; then read the directions aloud to the students.

The penguin is the perfect origami animal to use to enhance a unit on Australia, Antarctica or ocean life. By varying the size of the squares, you can create a family of penguins that can be placed on an ice floe (a table covered in white butcher paper).

 Fold a square piece of paper (8" x 8") in half diagonally.

 Fold down both sides as shown with dotted lines; then unfold fold made in step 1.

unfold

 Fold the wide angle up and the narrow angle down.

 Refold down center fold made in step 1.

 Lift up the head.

◇ Start Here!

Teacher: Read the instructions; then play the game with your students.

Copy and cut out the cards on pages 19–20. If you want to make the cards sturdier, glue them to card stock and laminate. Directions: Place the cards in a container; then have a student pull out a card and read the directions. All the students follow the directions, then the next card is read. Have the students begin sitting down. If your class is not yet ready for three- and four-step directions, refer to Listening Skills I and II Let's Get Moving cards.

Clap your hands twice, stand up, sit down.	Say "Hi," put your right hand on your left knee, turn around in a complete circle.
Stand up, hop once on both feet, sit down.	Put both thumbs on your nose, wiggle your fingers, then clap three times.
Whistle two notes, say the last three letters of the alphabet, then put both hands on top of your head.	Put your left hand on your right knee, put your right hand on your left knee, then say "Pretzel."
Spell RED backwards out loud, touch your toes, then say "Ouch!"	Close your eyes, point up, open your eyes.

Say "tweedle dee, tweedle dum," clap once, stand up, put your hands behind your back.

Touch your left baby finger to your chin, turn around once, hop once, say, "Apple."

Stand up, sit down, stand up, spell "sit" backwards.

Face the teacher's desk, face the classroom door, face the clock, hop on two feet three times.

Put both hands on your stomach, say "Yummy," clap once, clap twice.

Close your eyes, spell "cat" backwards aloud, open your eyes, say "Soda pop."

Say the answer to 5 + 5, stand up, sit down.

Put your right hand over your left eye, put your left hand over your right eye, say "I can't see," then clap 4 times.

◇ **Start Here!**

Teacher: Copy this page. Read the directions on page 31; then play the game with your students.

◇**Start Here!**

Teacher: See page 31 for directions.

It seems so easy to frown and harder to smile, but I heard it takes more work to frown. True or False?

You need to move 43 muscles to frown but only 17 muscles to smile. So if you want to relax, smile, smile, smile.

My friend gets very pale when she is scared. What causes this to happen?

When humans are frightened, their brains send messages to certain nerves that say, "Make the blood vessels under the skin get smaller." When blood is not flowing to the outer layers of skin, people get very pale and are less likely to bleed heavily if they are injured.

The brain doesn't know the difference between being frightened from a scary movie or from a person with a big knife. It only knows something frightening is happening and it needs to get blood away from the surface of the body as quickly as possible.

I like to listen to very loud music, but my mom says to turn down the sound before I go deaf. Could this really happen?

Smart mom! Even loud noises, such as fireworks or police sirens, heard for very short periods of time can cause minor hearing loss. A sense of dullness and ringing in the ears will soon go away if the noise stops. However, repeated loud noises, such as rock concerts, jet engines and your bedroom radio, will cause permanent hearing loss.

Yesterday, after running in a track meet, I got a bad pain in my side. My granny said it was just a stitch, and it would go away. What did she mean?

A stitch is a cramp in a muscle. When you run, your breathing rate increases. This causes the large muscle below your lungs to work extra hard. A poison, called lactic acid, builds up in this muscle, which causes it to feel tight and painful. By resting and breathing normally, the lactic acid is cleaned out of the muscle by the blood system and soon the stitch goes away.

I just cut my hair too short. How fast will it grow back?

Hair grows about five inches a year; it grows more in the summer than in the winter and more in the morning than at night.

Start Here!

Teacher: Read the instructions; then read the directions aloud to the students.

Hats have had many uses throughout history. They have represented military power: think of the green berets in Vietnam; safety: Steve Young's helmet on the football field; or cleanliness: the cap Florence Nightingale wore in her hospital.

These are just a few examples of the ways hats have been used by men and women alike.

This origami should be practiced on small scraps of paper, and when the students are ready, use large squares of butcher or bulletin board paper. A wonderful extension to this project is to have your students pick an interesting job and research headgear that is associated with that profession. Have them create their hat out of paper and have "Hat Day" in your class.

 Fold a large square of paper in half. The size will vary depending on the student's head. A general size would be about 30" X 30".

 Fold the left side towards the middle, starting at the top corner and ending at an imaginary point about one third of the way along the fold line.

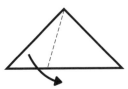

 Repeat with the right side.

 Fold the bottom left corner up along the fold line.

Fold the bottom right corner up along the fold line.

 Decorate and put it on your head!

◇ Start Here!

Teacher: Copy the accompanying picture. Then read the instructions and the story aloud to the students.

Denise was feeling lucky. Her teacher had just assigned everyone in her class to write a report on a favorite sea animal. Last spring her family had traveled to California to visit the Monterey Bay Aquarium, and Denise knew exactly what she was going to write about.

---

1 Large beds of giant kelp, a kind of seaweed, grow along the shoreline of Monterey, California. It is here you are likely to see a sea otter floating on its back. SEAWEED and SHORELINE are compound words. Write two COMPOUND WORDS below the giant kelp; then color the kelp BROWNISH-YEL-LOW.

2 About one hundred years ago the sea otter was almost extinct in California. The 50 or so otters left near Monterey were protected, and by 1940 there were several hundred sea otters. Color the two otter pups GRAY.

3 Otters are small sea mammals. They have unusually thick fur to keep them warm. Color the adult sea otter BROWN, leaving the patches around her face and stomach WHITE.

4 These playful creatures eat spiny sea urchins, clams, mussels, squid, starfish, crabs and sea cucumbers. (A sea cucumber is an animal that looks similar to the vegetable.) Sea otters have been photographed prying octopuses out of discarded soda cans floating in the ocean. Color the sea cucumber GREEN and the crab ORANGE.

5 When a pup gets separated from its mother, it is in danger of dying from the cold water or from starvation, since an otter pup can't hunt for itself. Color the top of the ocean water BLUE.

6 At the Monterey Bay Aquarium, lost pups are raised by expert caretakers with the goal of returning the otters to the wild. The babies are fed a "clam shake" consisting of clams, squid, half-and-half, fish oil, vitamins and minerals. Color the clams' shells BROWN and the squid GRAY.

7 The otter pups need to be taught how to find seafood and break it open with a rock. Trained ocean divers act as the pups' mothers, teaching them everything they need to know to survive in Monterey Bay. Color the rocks BLACK. Then count how many rocks there are, and write your answer in the bottom left-hand corner.

8 A diver and his assigned pup hunt for shelled animals in the aquarium's Great Tide Pool, being sure to select a pounding rock. Rolling over on his back next to a floating pup, the diver shows the otter how to whack the rock on the hard shell and remove a tasty snack. Soon, the pup can hunt on its own. Color the starfish RED. Then write a word that rhymes with POUND in the top left-hand corner.

Saving an Otter Pup

Name _____   Date _____

adult otter

otter pup

squid

kelp

sea
cucumber

crab

clam

◇ **Start Here!**

Teacher: Copy the accompanying picture. Then read the instructions and the story aloud to the students.

"Mom, I have a math test tomorrow. Can you help me practice?" asked Denise.
"Sure! What are you studying right now?" said Mom.
"It's one of those tests where the teacher reads the questions aloud. Those types of tests always make me nervous, and this one will have lots of fractions," said Denise.
"Just relax. Use good listening skills and you'll do great."

1 ▷ Find three spheres, or balls, and color them BROWN.

2 ▷ Solve the addition problem on the right side of the chalkboard.

3 ▷ Circle the THIRD, SEVENTEENTH and TWENTY-FIRST letters of the alphabet.

4 ▷ What does four sets of six equal? Write your answer on the front of the desk.

5 ▷ Solve the SUBTRACTION PROBLEM on the left side of the chalkboard.

6 ▷ Color one windowpane BLUE to show one-fourth.

7 ▷ The Smith family had one whole apple pie. Dad cut it into six pieces. If two pieces get eaten, how many pieces are left? Write your answer under the apples.

8 ▷ Color one-third of the books in the bookcase ORANGE, color one-third PURPLE and one-third GREEN.

9 ▷ How many spheres, or balls, are not colored? Write your answer on the bottom left-hand corner of your paper.

10 ▷ If two children split 14 pieces of candy equally, how many pieces will each child get? Circle the correct answer on the board.

11 ▷ Color three of the five flowers to show three-fifths.

12 ▷ Color two of the three pencils in the pencil box to show two-thirds.

13 ▷ Shade in one-half of the alphabet YELLOW.

14 ▷ Color four of the apples on the teacher's desk RED.

Name _____ Date_____

abcdefghijklmnopqrstuvwxyz

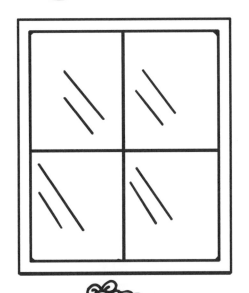

```
  93              93
- 47    6 pieces  - 47
        7 pieces
  47    8 pieces    47
+ 93            + 93
```

◇ **Start Here!**

Teacher: Read the instructions and the story aloud to the students.

"Who are you studying for your famous American report?" asked Denise. She and her best friend were sitting on her bedroom floor painting their toenails red.

"I don't know yet," her friend replied. "But I bet you know who you're writing about."

"Benjamin Franklin," said Denise. "I like the crazy way he proved lightning was the same thing as electricity."

1 Benjamin Franklin was born in Boston, Massachusetts, about 300 years ago. He was the 15th of 17 children. He would grow up to become one of the most famous Americans to ever live. Write 15 in the lower right-hand corner of the paper.

2 When Ben was a young boy the United States of America was still part of Great Britain. There were no free public schools like there are today. Ben's parents had enough money to send him to school for only two years. Write FREE SCHOOL above the building's doorway.

3 By the time he was ten years old, he was spending his days working in his father's candle- and soap-making shop. At age 12 Ben started helping his older brother, James, who was a printer. Here Ben learned about printing books and newspapers. Write the number 12 on the newspaper.

4 Each year Ben Franklin wrote a book called <u>Poor Richard's Almanac</u>. An almanac is a book that gives the best dates for planting crops, the cycles of the moon and tides, along with yearly holidays and interesting sayings such as "a penny saved is a penny earned." Draw the moon in the top right-hand corner of the picture.

5 At age 36 Ben Franklin invented the Franklin stove. Made of iron, it was a safer way to heat homes than other fireplaces. Because of Franklin's stove, fewer people died in house fires, and it lead the way to the development of the gas furnaces that now heat most American homes. Color the logs BROWN and the flames RED and ORANGE.

6 Franklin also invented bifocal glasses. These glasses helped people see both near and far. Color the top of Ben's glasses BLUE and the bottom of his glasses RED.

7 His most famous experiment involved a kite. It had a pointed metal tip, along with a metal key tied to the kite's tail. Franklin flew the kite in a storm. When lightning struck the kite, Ben touched the metal key and felt a shock. This was the first proof that lightning and electricity were the same thing. (Do not try this experiment at home. It is very dangerous.) Color the lightning bolt and electric shock waves YELLOW.

Name _____ Date _____

◇**Start Here!**

Teacher: Read the instructions and the story aloud to the students.

I'm going to give you a piece of paper. When you get it, write your first and last name on the top line. Next, write the numbers 1–7 down the left-hand side of the paper. Then, put your pencil down and get ready to listen to a true story.

Almost 150 years ago a terrible war raged through our country. The question of whether Southerners had the right to keep others as slaves was a main reason for the war. The Northern states felt strongly that slavery was wrong. However, the South, which was covered in huge plantations, felt that slaves were needed to help plant and pick their main crop, cotton.

In 1861, 11 of the 33 states left the Union and became a new country called the Confederate States of America. In April of that year, Southern battleships attacked Northern battleships at Fort Sumter, near Charleston, South Carolina. The Civil War had started. It would last for four years.

In 1863, a massive battle was fought near the town of Gettysburg, Pennsylvania. Over 50,000 men from both North and South were killed or wounded. Some who died were boys as young as ten, whose job was to carry ammunition for the older riflemen. Four months later, while the war was still being fought, Abraham Lincoln, then president of the United States, traveled to the site of the Battle of Gettysburg. There he gave a speech that is now known as the Gettysburg Address.

In his speech he reminded Americans that the United States had been started with the idea that "all men were created equal" and had a right to liberty, or freedom. Lincoln called the fields of Gettysburg "a final resting place for those who died here, that our nation might live." His simple words helped the Northern troops take courage, and in 1865, after many more battles, the South agreed to rejoin the United States. Slavery was no more!

Listen closely as I read each question; then write the letter that gives the best answer.

1. About how many years ago was the Civil War fought?   A. 50 years   B. 150 years   C. 500 years

2. What was one of the reasons the North and South went to war?   A. The North wanted more money.
B. Northerners didn't like wearing cotton.   C. Northerners didn't like slavery.

3. At the Battle of Gettysburg, about how many boys and men were killed or injured?
A. 50,000   B. 5,000   C. 500

4. What were young boys doing in the middle of such a horrible fight?
A. driving wagons full of supplies   B. helping the wounded   C. carrying ammunition

5. What did Lincoln mean when he called Gettysburg "a final resting place for those who died here"?
A. It was a cemetery for soldiers.   B. It was a hotel for soldiers.
C. It was a place for the soldiers to take a break.

6. Liberty means: A. a statue   B. freedom   C. the name of a rock band

7. Write a new title for "The Civil War." _____

Page 10: Questions Kids Ask

Have the children number a piece of paper from 1–8. Then ask them the following questions after each story.

Why do I sneeze?

1. Sneezing gets rid of
   A. dust   B. germs   C. both dust and germs
2. When you sneeze, how fast does the air move out of your nose?
   A. 50 mph   B. 100 mph   C. 80 mph

What is a germ?

3. What do you need to see a germ?   A. a magnifying glass   B. a telescope   C. a microscope
4. You should cover your nose when you sneeze because: A. You might be sneezing out germs.
   B. It's embarrassing to sneeze in front of your friends.   C. Your teacher told you to do it.

Why do I have a bellybutton?

5. The tube, or umbilical cord, brings what to the unborn baby?   A. pizza   B. oxygen and nutrients   C. electricity
6. The umbilical cord joins a baby to its
   A. mother   B. father   C. doctor

Why do I have skin?

7. Skin keeps what where?   A. your insides out   B. your insides in   C. the outside in
8. Why does your skin have pores?
   A. to keep your body cool   B. to let germs in
   C. to hold nerve endings

Page 21: Telling Time

Read the following questions to your students while they use the clock faces on page 21 for their answers.

1. Fill in clock #4 so it shows seven o'clock.
2. On clock #9 show what time it will be one hour after 3:20.
3. On clock #1 show what time your school day starts.
4. Put the hands on clock #5 so it shows 1:05.
5. Make clock #8 read midnight or noon.
6. Show half past three on clock #2.
7. Show what time it would be one hour before 9:45 on clock #7.
8. Show quarter past twelve on clock #3.
9. Show what time you go to lunch recess on clock #6.

Page 22: More Questions Kids Ask

Have the children number a piece of paper from 1–10. Then ask them the following questions after each story.

Frown or Smile?

1. How many muscles do you use to smile?
   A. 34   B. 43   C. 17
2. How many muscles do you use to frown?
   A. 34   B. 43   C. 17

Pale Friend

3. When you are frightened, what do the blood vessels under the skin do?
   A. widen   B. shrink   C. stay the same
4. Why is it important to get blood away from the surface of your body when there is danger?
   A. Pale skin frightens enemies.
   B. Less blood will be lost if your skin gets cut.
   C. so you sweat less

Loud Music

5. What best describes how ears feel after being exposed to loud music: A. dull and ringing   B. clear but ringing   C. the same as usual.
6. Can a loud radio or concert music cause hearing loss?   A. yes   B. no

It's a Stitch

7. A stitch in this paragraph means:
   A. a piece of thread   B. someone who tattletales   C. a cramp
8. Which of the following is a poison that can build up in your muscles?
   A. lactic acid   B. battery acid   C. stomach acid

Hair

9. About how long does your hair grow each year?   A. 3 inches   B. 4 inches   C. 5 inches
10. When will you grow the most hair?
    A. during a winter night   B. during a summer morning   C. during a summer night

Answer Page

Page 8: Alexander Graham Bell

1. C. Inventing the telephone
2. A. Scotland
3. B. Watson
4. A. steel rods and electrical wire
5. B. deaf
6. B. 75 years old
7. Answers will vary.

Page 10: Questions Kids Ask

Why do I sneeze?

1. C. both dust and germs
2. B. 100 mph

What is a germ?

3. C. a microscope
4. A. You might be sneezing out germs.

Why do I have a bellybutton?

5. B. oxygen and nutrients
6. A. mother

Why do I have skin?

7. B. your insides in
8. A. to keep your body cool

Page 11: Ludwig van Beethoven

1. C. grumpy
2. B. Mozart
3. A. sloppy, messy, talented
4. C. 30,000
5. B. by writing in a notebook
6. A. Vienna
7. Answers will vary.

Page 15: The Deadly Touch

1. B. hunger
2. C. Hollyhock
3. A. because he dreamt all night
4. C. a sad look
5. B. a stranger
6. A. They turned to gold.
7. Answers will vary.

Page 22: More Question Kids Ask

Frown or smile?

1. C. 17
2. B. 43

Pale friend

3. B. shrink
4. B. Less blood will be lost if your skin gets cut.

Loud music

5. A. dull and ringing
6. A. yes

It's a Stitch

7. C. a cramp
8. A. lactic acid

Hair

9. C. 5 inches
10. B. during a summer morning

Page 30: The Civil War

1. B. 150 years
2. C. Northerners didn't like slavery.
3. A. 50,000
4. C. carrying ammunition
5. A. It was a cemetery for soldiers.
   B. freedom
6. Answers will vary.

© Rainbow Bridge Publishing   www.rbpbooks.com   reproducible   MBS—Listening Skills Grade 3

Rainbow Bridge Publishing
Certificate
of Completion

Awarded to

_____

for the completion of

Mastering Basic Skills

George Stark.

_____   _____
Publisher's Signature   Parent's Signature

Receive RBP's FREE Parent and Teacher on-line newsletter!

Receive special offers, FREE learning exercises and great ideas to use in your classroom and at home!

To receive our on-line newsletter, please provide us with the following information:

Name:_____

Address:_____

City:_____ State: ___ Zip: _____

Email Address:_____

Store where book was purchased: _____

Child's grade level: _____

Book title purchased: _____

Or visit our website:

www.sbakids.com

Or Call:
801-268-8887

Summer Bridge Activities™

Title	Price
Grade P-K	$12.95
Grade K-1	$12.95
Grade 1-2	$12.95
Grade 2-3	$12.95
Grade 3-4	$12.95
Grade 4-5	$12.95
Grade 5-6	$12.95

Summer Bridge Middle School™

Title	Price
Grade 6-7	$12.95
Grade 7-8	$12.95

Summer Bridge Reading Activities™

Title	Price
Grade 1-2	$6.95
Grade 2-3	$6.95
Grade 3-4	$6.95

Summer Journal™

Title	Price
Summer Journal™	$4.95

Summer Dailies™

Title	Price
Summer Dailies™	$4.95

Summer Traveler™

Title	Price
Summer Traveler™	$4.95

Math Bridge™

Title	Price
Grade 1	$9.95
Grade 2	$9.95
Grade 3	$9.95
Grade 4	$9.95
Grade 5	$9.95
Grade 6	$9.95
Grade 7	$9.95
Grade 8	$9.95

Reading Bridge™

Title	Price
Grade 1	$9.95
Grade 2	$9.95
Grade 3	$9.95
Grade 4	$9.95
Grade 5	$9.95
Grade 6	$9.95
Grade 7	$9.95
Grade 8	$9.95

Skill Builders™

Title	Price
Phonics Grade 1	$2.50
Spelling Grade 2	$2.50
Vocabulary Grade 3	$2.50
Reading Grade 1	$2.50
Reading Grade 2	$2.50
Reading Grade 3	$2.50
Math Grade 1	$2.50
Math Grade 2	$2.50
Math Grade 3	$2.50
Subtraction Grade 1	$2.50
Subtraction Grade 2	$2.50
Multiplication Grade 3	$2.50

Connection Series™

Title	Price
Reading Grade 1	$10.95
Reading Grade 2	$10.95
Reading Grade 3	$10.95
Math Grade 1	$10.95
Math Grade 2	$10.95
Math Grade 3	$10.95

Mastering Basic Skills™

Title	Price
Grammar Grade 1	$5.95
Grammar Grade 2	$5.95
Grammar Grade 3	$5.95
Word Problems Grade 1	$4.95
Word Problems Grade 2	$4.95
Word Problems Grade 3	$4.95
Word Problems Grade 4	$4.95
Listening Skills Grade 1	$4.95
Listening Skills Grade 2	$4.95
Listening Skills Grade 3	$4.95

Math Test Preparation™

Title	Price
Math Test Prep Grade 1	$10.95
Math Test Prep Grade 2	$10.95
Math Test Prep Grade 3	$10.95

First Step Spanish™

Title	Price
Colors/Shapes	$5.95
Alphabet/Numbers	$5.95

Available everywhere!
Visit your favorite bookstore.

Place Proper Postage Here

Rainbow Bridge Publishing
PO Box 571470
Salt Lake City, Utah 84157

Keeping Children Busy, Happy, and Learning During the Summer and Beyond!